RECORDED VERSIONS
GUITAR

**AUTHENTIC TRANSCRIPTIONS
WITH NOTES AND TABLATURE**

**Transcribed by
Jesse Gress**

eric clapton
unplugged

D1463567

RECORDED VERSIONS
GUITAR

AUTHENTIC TRANSCRIPTIONS
WITH NOTES AND TABLATURE

**Transcribed by
Jesse Gress**

eric clapton unplugged

Important Notice

Exclusive Distributors for
THE WORLD excluding U.S.A & Canada
Music Sales Limited
14-15 Berners Street
London W1T 3LJ.

Music Sales Pty Limited
20 Resolution Drive,
Caringbah, NSW 2229, Australia.

Order No AM91067
ISBN 0-7119-3391-X
This book © copyright 1993 by Wise Publications

eric clapton unplugged contents

Alberta

Words and Music by Huddie Ledbetter

1st, 2nd, 3rd and 4th Verses

(2, 3, 4. See additional lyrics)

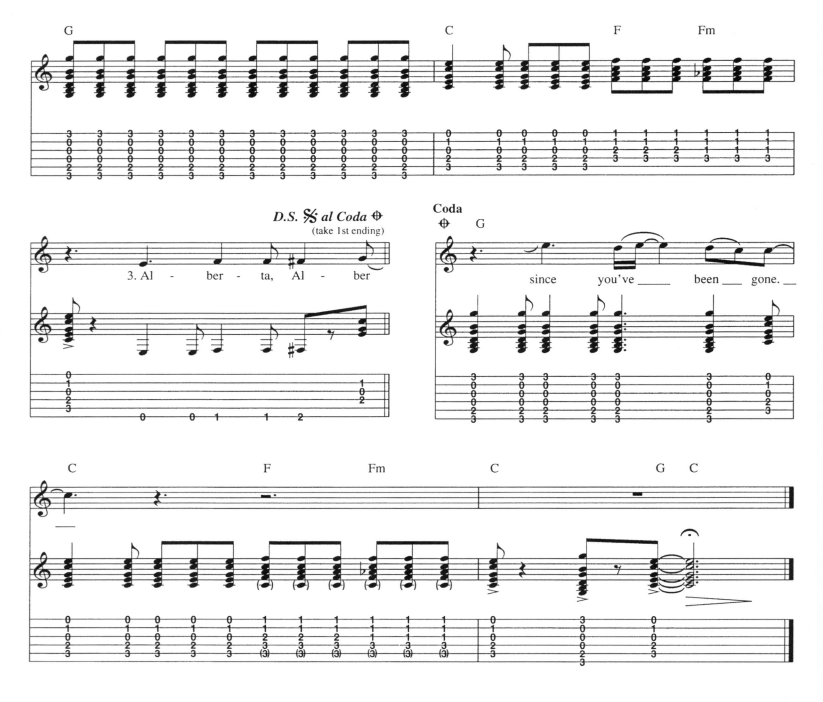

Additional lyrics

2. Alberta, Alberta, where'd you stay last night?
   Alberta, Alberta, where'd you stay last night?
   Come home this mornin', clothes don't fit you right.

3. Alberta, Alberta, girl you're on my mind.
   Alberta, Alberta, girl you're on my mind.
   Ain't had no lovin' in such a great, long time.

4. Alberta, Alberta, where you been so long?
   Alberta, Alberta, where you been so long?
   Ain't had no lovin' since you've been gone.

Before You Accuse Me

Words and Music by Eugene McDaniels

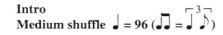

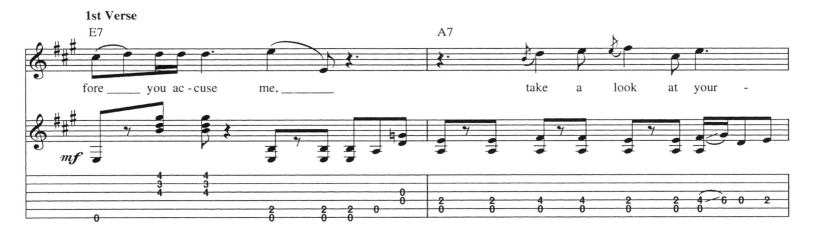

Guitar Solo

2nd Guitar Solo

Hey Hey

By William "Big Bill" Broonzy

Intro

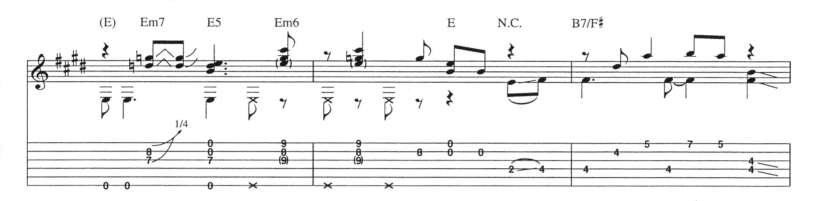

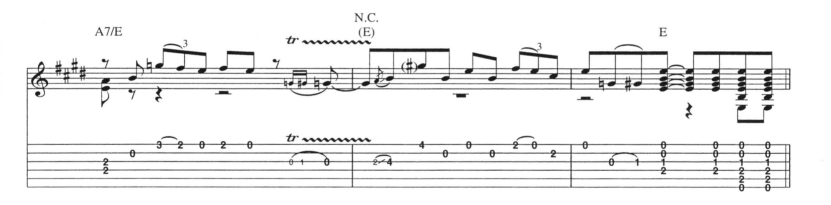

2nd Verse

Hey, hey, ___ hey, hey ___ ba - by, hey. _____

Layla

Words and Music by Eric Clapton and Jim Gordon

2nd and 3rd Verses

2. Tried to give you _ con-sol - a - tion, __ your old man had let you
3. Make the best of the sit-u - a - tion, __ before I fin - ally go in-

down. __ Like _ a _ fool, I fall in love _ with you.
sane. __ Please _ don't say we'll nev-er find _ a way.

Tom (6)

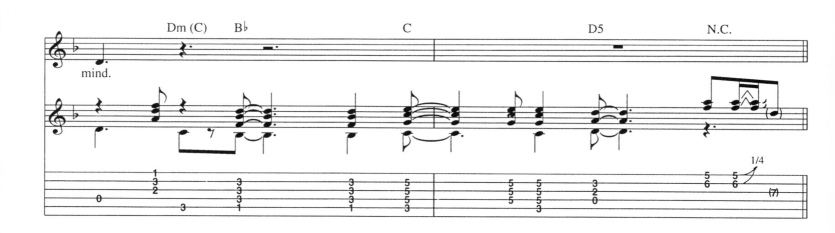

Guitar Solo

Malted Milk
Words and Music by Robert Johnson

Intro

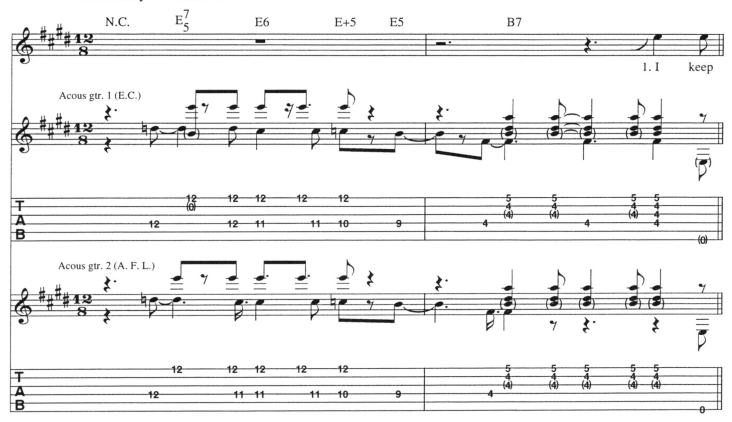

Ba - by,
fix me _____ one more drink 'n' hug your dad - dy one ____ more time. ____
Keep on stir - rin'

even bend

An' I have a

fun - ny, fun - ny feel - in', ___ and the hair ___ ris - in' on ___ my head. __

Free time

43

Lonely Stranger

Words and Music by Eric Clapton

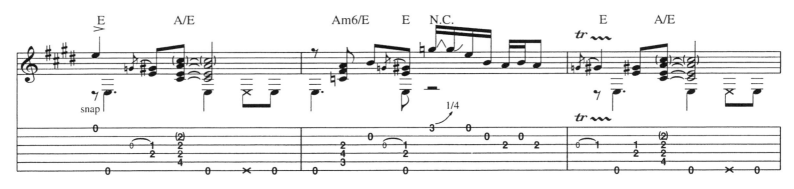

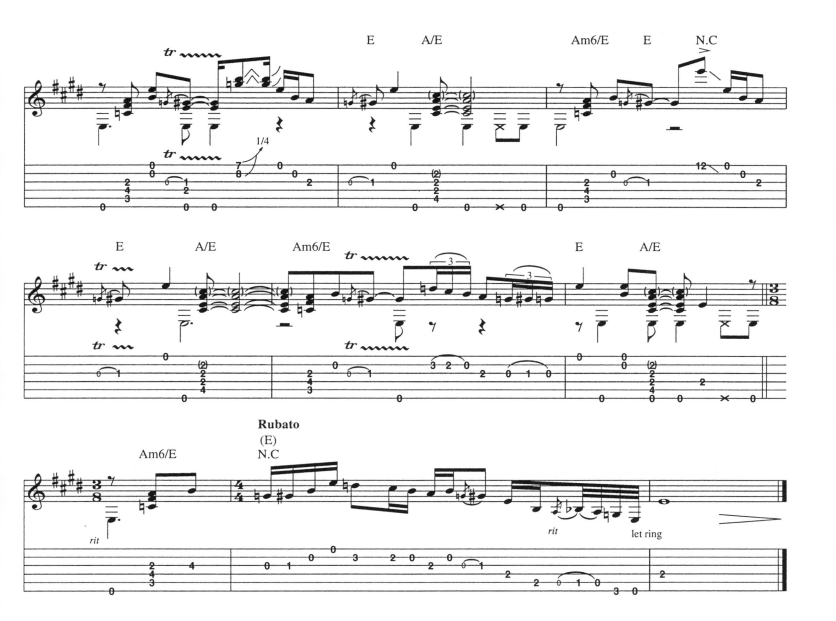

Additional Lyrics

2. I was born with a raging thirst,
   A hunger to be free.
   But I've learned through the years,
   Don't encourage me.

3. When I walk, stay behind,
   Don't get close to me.
   'Cause it's sure to end in tears,
   So just let me be.

4. Some will say that I'm no good,
   Maybe I agree.
   Take a look, then walk away,
   That's alright with me.

Nobody Knows You When You're Down and Out

Words and Music by Jimmy Cox

Old Love

Words and Music by Eric Clapton and Robert Cray

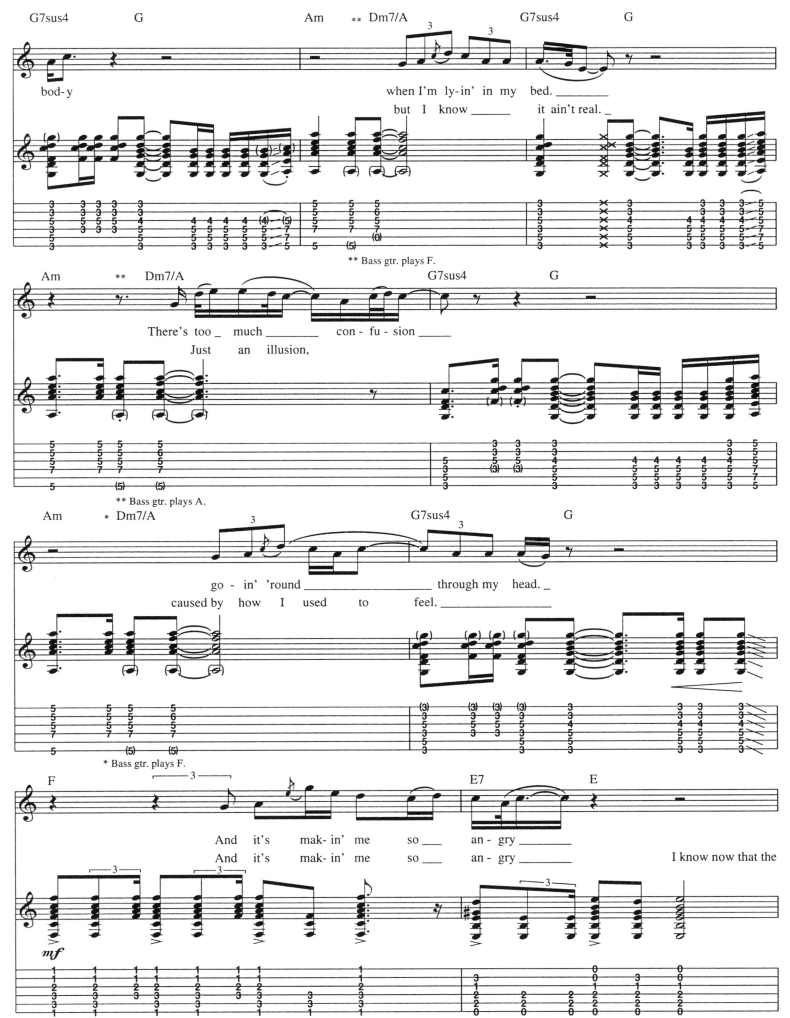

* Bass gtr. plays D throughout chords.

Rollin' and Tumblin'

Written by Muddy Waters

Moderately fast ♩ = 122

1st Verse

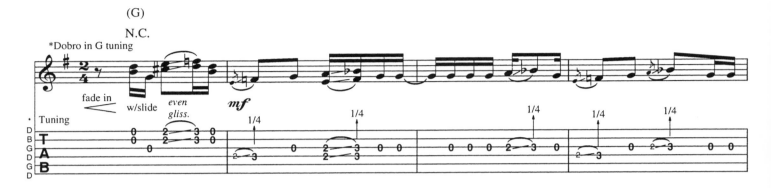

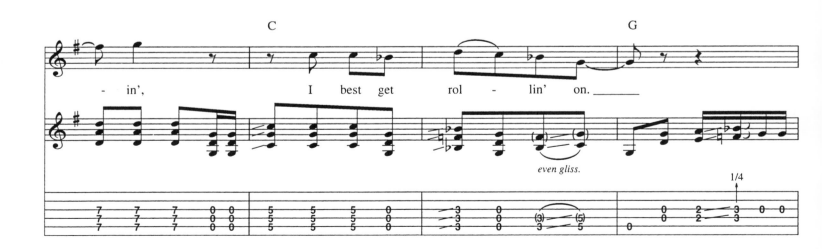

2nd Verse

2. Well now, come here ba - by,

sit down on dad - dy's knee. _____

Well now, come here ba-

Guitar solo

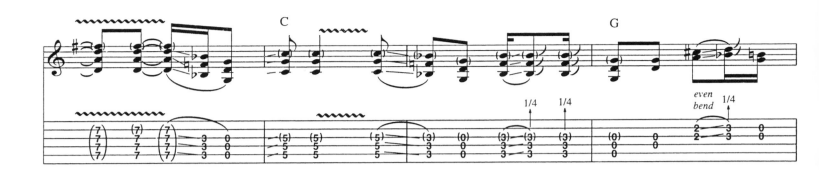

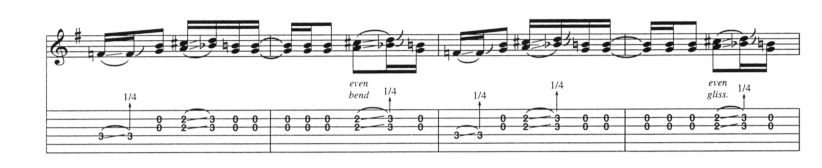

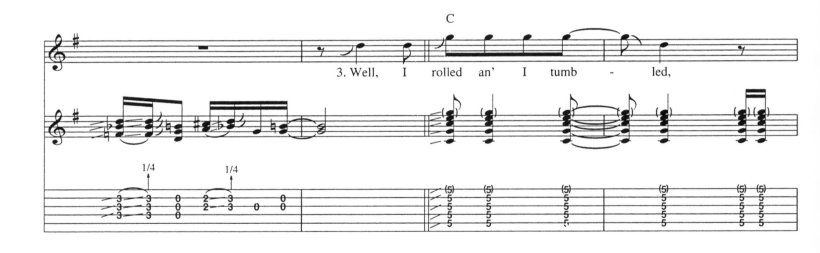

3. Well, I rolled an' I tumb - led,

cried the whole __ night long. _____

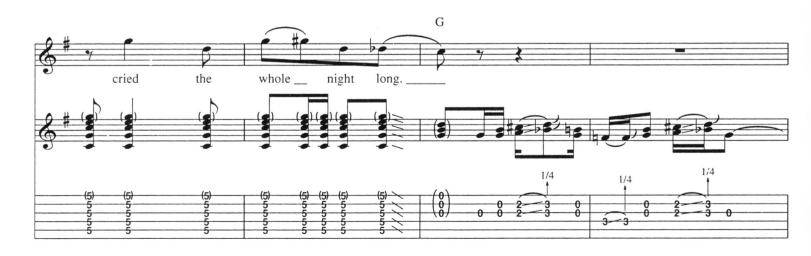

4th Verse

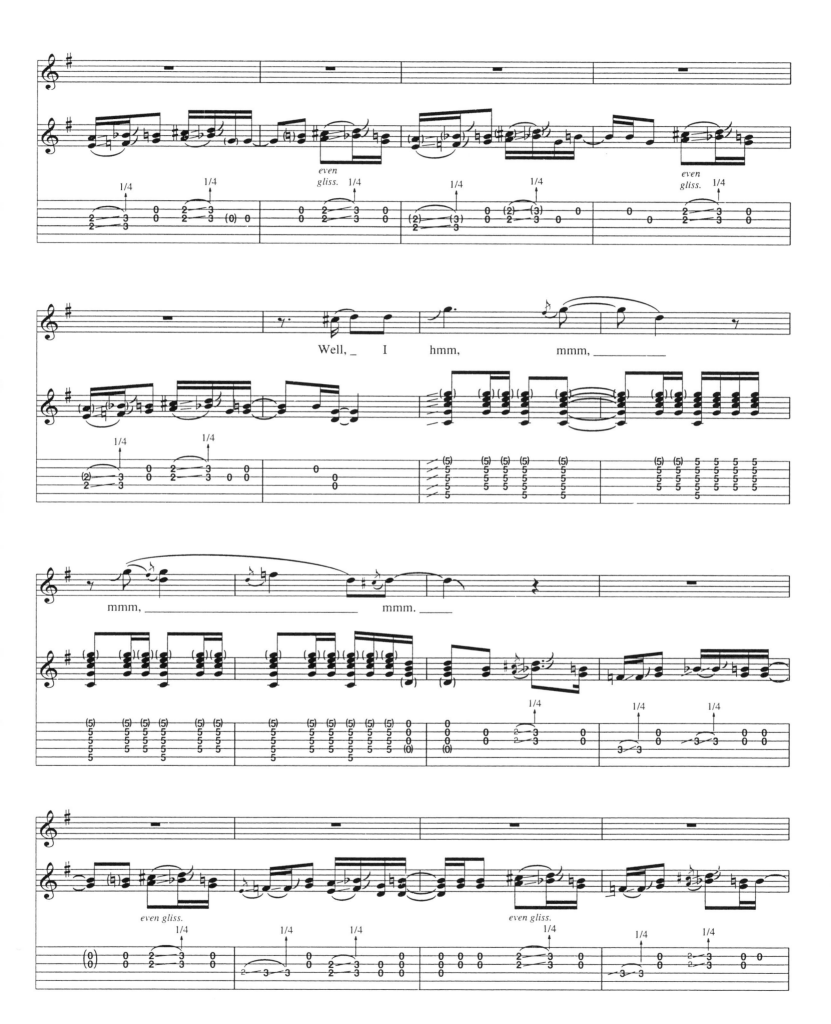

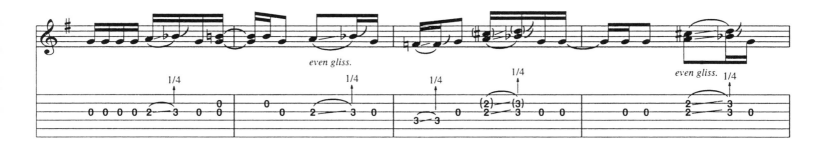

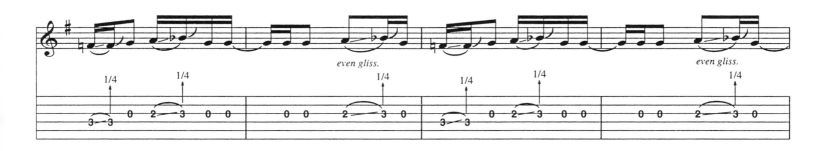

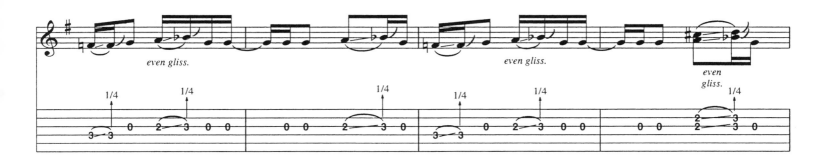

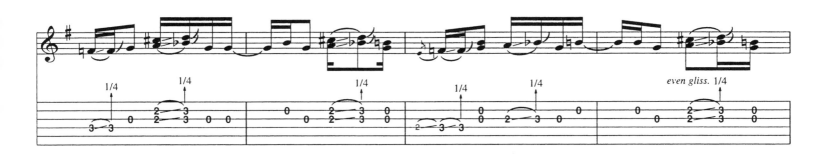

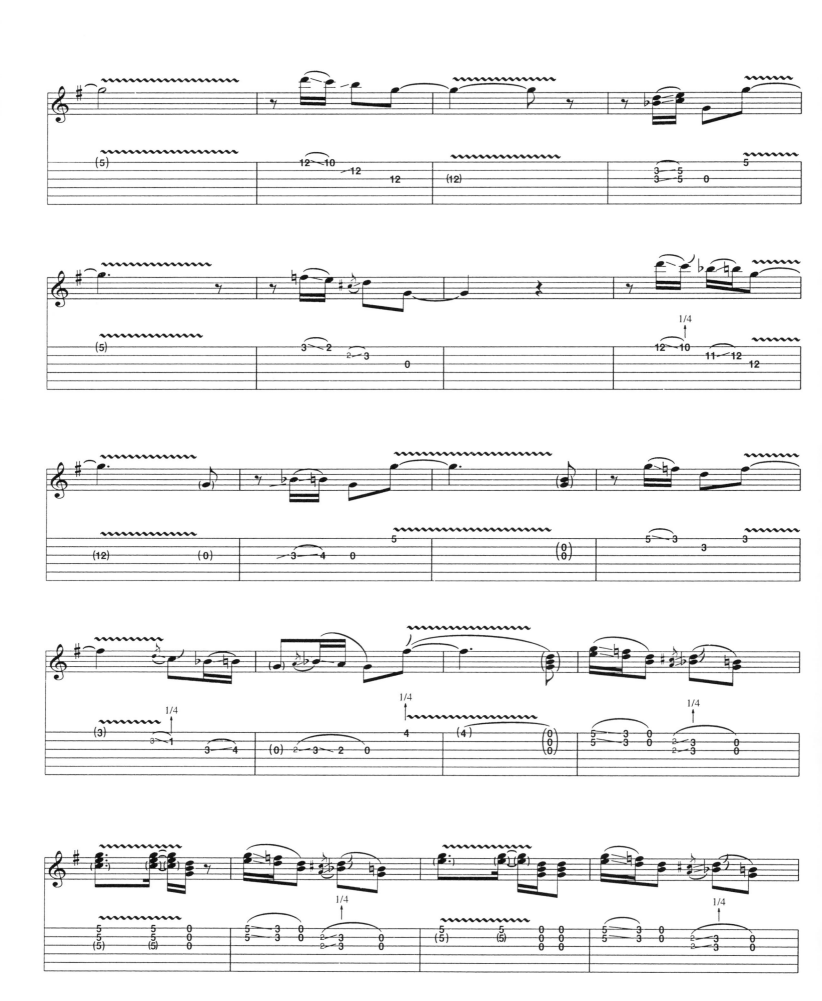

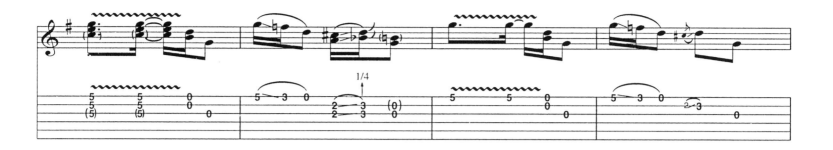

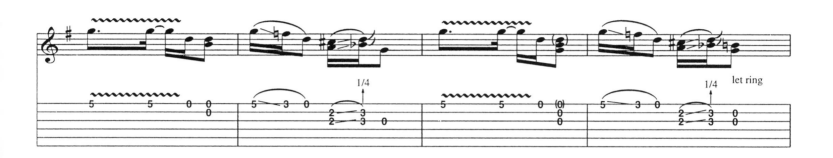

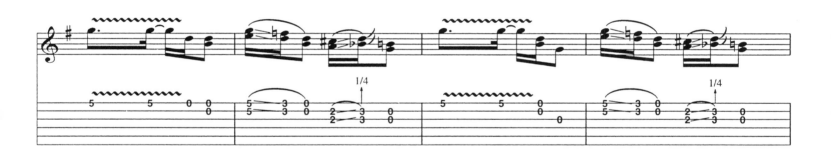

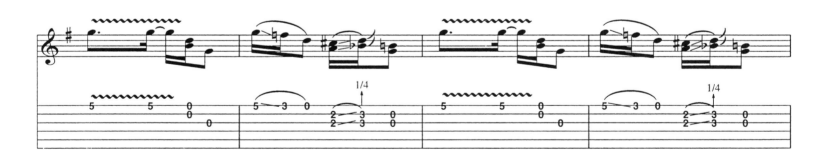

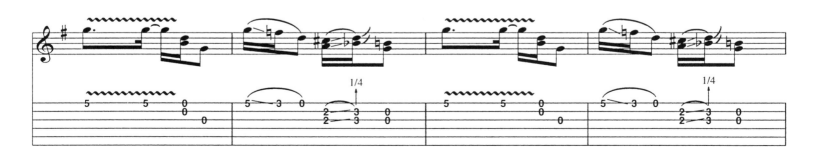

Running On Faith

Words and Music by Jerry Lynn Williams

Bridge

But __ I've __ al-ways been

one to take each ____ and ev-'ry day. ___

Seems like __ by _

now __ I'd find a love who would care, _____ yeah just for me. _____

D.S. 𝄋 al Coda ⊕

even gliss   let ring   let ring

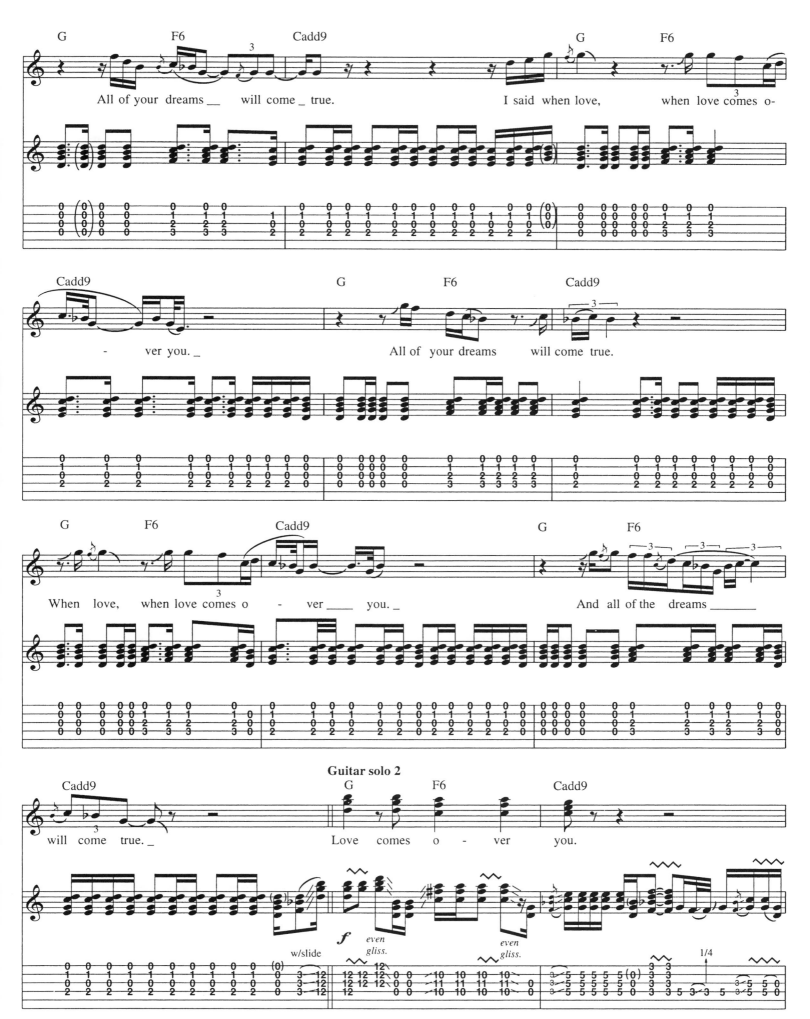

Signe

Words and Music by Eric Clapton

Intro

Moderately fast bossa nova feel ♩ = 176

* T on ⑥--

* T = Thumb

Tears In Heaven

Words and Music by Eric Clapton and Will Jennings

Time can bring ya down, _____ time can bend your knees. _

Time can break your heart __

_ have ya beg - gin' please, _____ beg-gin' please. _____

Walkin' Blues

Words and Music by Robert Johnson

Guitar Solo

3rd Verse

Guitar Solo 2

103

San Francisco Bay Blues

Words and Music by Jesse Fuller

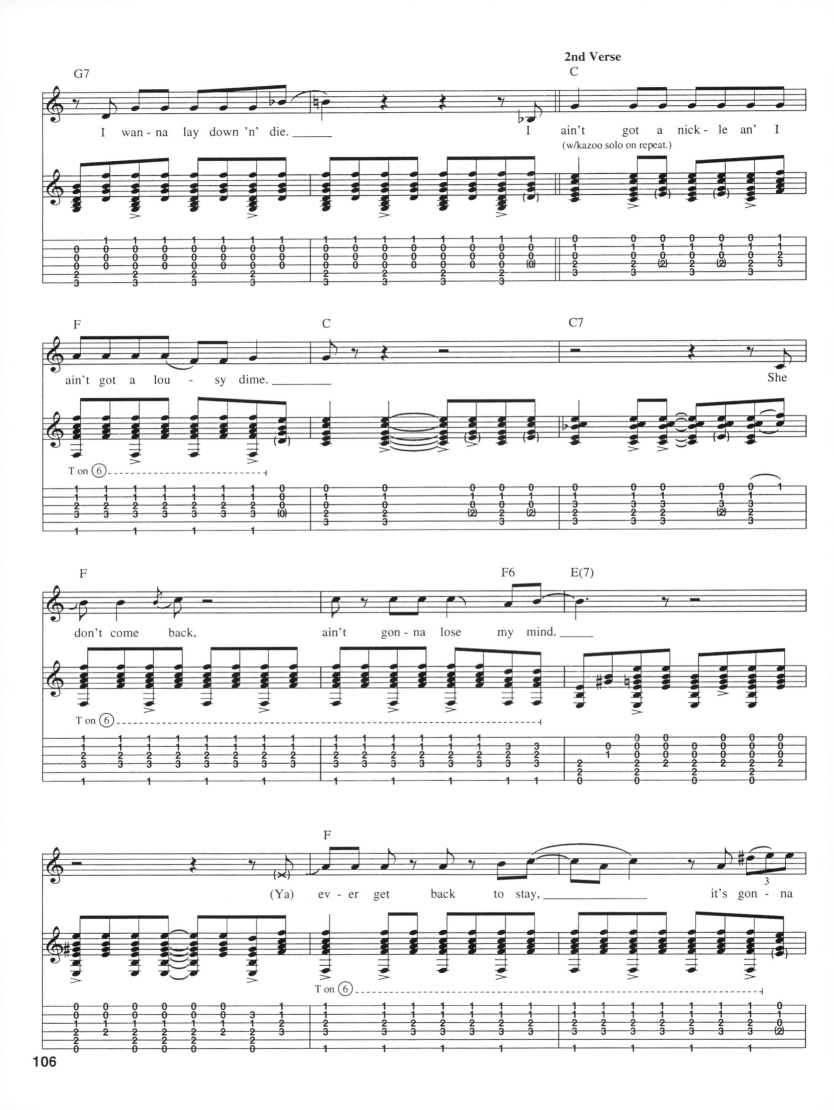

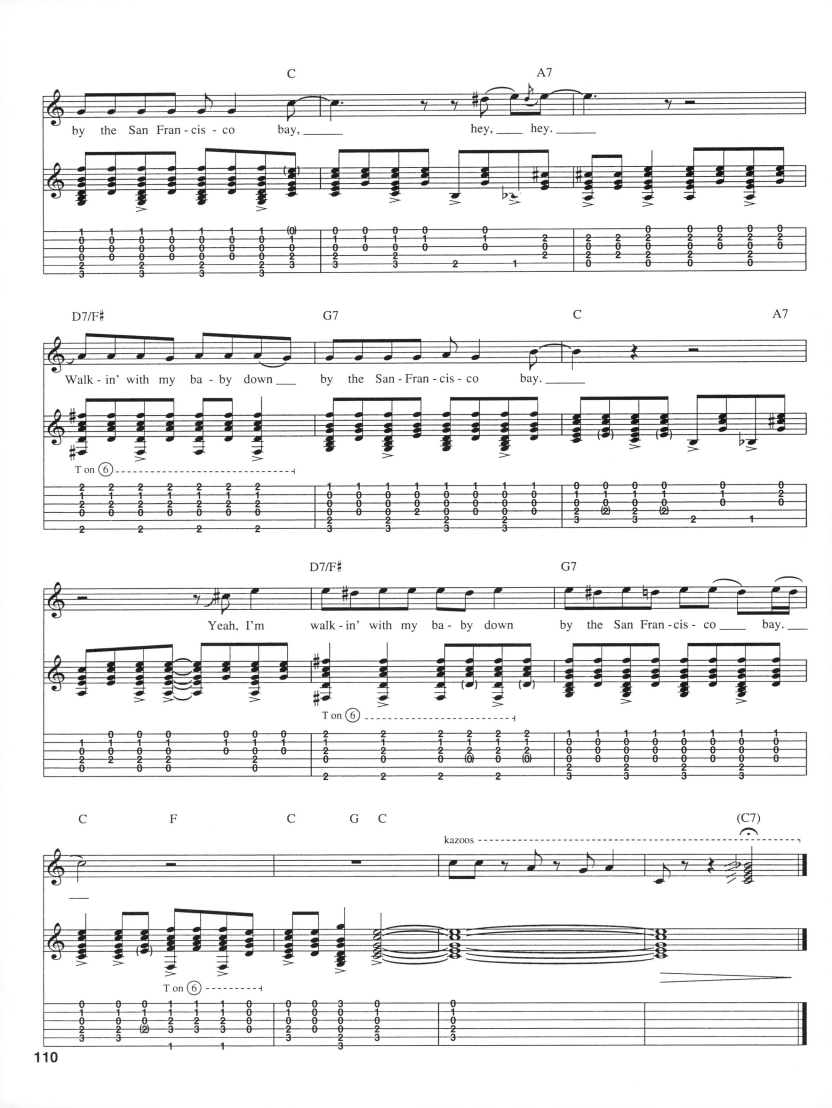

NOTATION LEGEND

Printed in the EU   02/14(189583)